Trader's Mindset: The Key to Success for Financial Freedom

FRANCO ARÉVALO

CONTENTS

1 Introduction to the Emotional Connection with Money

Money is a powerful force that can have a deep emotional impact on us. Whether we have a lot of it or very little, our relationship with money can be complex and multifaceted. It can bring us joy, security, and a sense of accomplishment, but it can also create stress, anxiety, and feelings of inadequacy. In order to truly understand and manage our finances effectively, it is important to recognize the emotional connection we have with money and how it can influence our thoughts and behaviors.

One way in which we can develop a healthy emotional connection with money is by understanding our personal values and priorities. What is most important to us in life? How do we want to use our money to support those values? By aligning our spending and saving habits with our values, we can feel more fulfilled and satisfied with

Another important aspect of our emotional connection with money is our attitude and mindset towards it. Do we view money as a means to an end, or do we put a lot of value on accumulating wealth for its own sake? Do we see money as a source of stress or a tool for creating positive change in our lives? Our attitudes towards money can have a significant impact on our financial behaviors and outcomes.

Finally, it is important to recognize that our emotional connection with money is not just about our individual feelings, but also about the societal and cultural influences that shape our relationship with it. From a young age, we are taught certain beliefs and values about money through our families, communities, and media. These external influences can shape our financial habits and attitudes in both positive and negative ways.

In this chapter, we will explore the various ways in which our emotional connection with money can influence our financial lives. By understanding and managing these emotional factors, we can create a more positive and fulfilling relationship with money.

Spending habits: Our emotions can often drive our spending decisions, whether it be impulsive buying to satisfy a desire or overspending to keep up with others. By understanding our emotional triggers for spending, we can make more mindful and balanced financial choices.

Savings and investment decisions: Our emotional connection to money can also impact how we approach saving and investing. For example, fear of loss may prevent us from taking on financial risk, while a desire for security may lead us to be more conservative with our investments.

Debt management: Our emotional connection to money can affect how we manage debt. For example, feelings of shame or inadequacy may prevent us from seeking help with debt management, while feelings of anxiety may lead us to overspend in an attempt to feel financially secure.

Career and job satisfaction: Our emotional connection to money can also impact our career and job satisfaction. If we feel like we are not being fairly compensated or that our financial needs are not being met, it can lead to feelings of frustration and dissatisfaction in our work.

Relationship dynamics: Our emotional connection to money can also influence our relationships, both personally and professionally. For example, differing attitudes towards money management can lead to conflicts within a romantic relationship, while a focus on wealth and status may affect our relationships with colleagues and friends.

Managing our emotions can help us create a more positive and satisfying relationship with money. By understanding our emotional triggers and how they influence our financial decisions, we can make more mindful and balanced choices. This can lead to a greater sense of financial control and well-being, as well as reduced stress and anxiety around money.

Managing our emotions can also help us set and achieve financial goals that align with our values and priorities. When we are able to recognize and address any negative emotional patterns around money, we can make progress towards financial stability and security.

Additionally, managing our emotions can help improve our relationships with others, particularly when it comes to financial matters. By being aware of and addressing any emotional issues that may be causing conflicts or misunderstandings, we can create a more positive and supportive environment for financial decision-making and communication. Overall, managing our emotions can help us create a more positive and satisfying relationship with money.

2 Negative emotions associated with money: fear, greed, guilt, shame

Negative emotions associated with money can have a powerful impact on our financial lives and decision-making. Fear, greed, guilt, and shame are all common emotions that can arise when we are dealing with money, and they can lead us down a path of poor financial decisions or even financial ruin.

One of the most common negative emotions associated with money is fear. This fear can manifest in many different ways and can be triggered by a variety of factors. Some people may fear that they will never have enough money, while others may fear that they will lose the money they have.

One of the primary sources of fear when it comes to money is the fear of not having enough. This fear can be fueled by a lack of financial stability or security, as well as by the constant pressure to keep up with others. It can lead to feelings of inadequacy and a constant need to prove oneself, which can be exhausting and demoralizing.

Another source of fear related to money is the fear of losing what one has. This can be due to factors such as market fluctuations, unexpected expenses, or a lack of planning. It can lead to a constant worry about the future and a tendency to hold onto money tightly, rather than taking calculated risks.

In addition to these fears, there is also the fear of not being able to afford the things that one wants or needs. This can lead to feelings of frustration and resentment, as well as a constant craving for more.

Fear is a natural emotion when it comes to money, but it is important to remember that it is only one aspect of the financial picture. By acknowledging and addressing these fears, we can work towards a more balanced and healthy relationship with money.

Greed is a negative emotion that is closely associated with money. It is the intense desire to acquire more wealth or possessions, often at the expense of others. People who are greedy are willing to do whatever it takes to get what they want, regardless of the consequences or the harm it may cause to others.

Greed can lead to a number of negative outcomes, both for the person experiencing it and for those around them. For example, greedy people may engage in unethical or illegal activities in order to get ahead financially. They may lie, cheat, or steal in order to get what they want. This can lead to legal problems and social ostracism, as well as damage to relationships and reputation.

Greed can also lead to a lack of empathy and compassion towards others. Greedy people may be more focused on their own needs and desires, rather than considering the well-being of others. This can lead to selfish behavior and a lack of concern for the welfare of others.

Greed can also lead to a lack of balance in one's life. People who are greedy may become so focused on acquiring more wealth and possessions that they neglect other important areas of their life, such as family, friends, and personal well-being. This can lead to feelings of loneliness, isolation, and dissatisfaction with life.

Greed is a negative emotion that can have serious consequences for both the person experiencing it and for those around them. It is important to recognize and address greed in order to avoid the negative outcomes that it can bring.

Guilt is a feeling of responsibility or remorse for something we have done wrong. When it comes to money, guilt may be felt when we spend more than we can afford, or when we feel like we have not lived up to our financial responsibilities. This guilt can lead to anxiety and stress, as we try to make up for our mistakes and avoid feeling guilty again.

Shame is a feeling of dishonor or disgrace. When it comes to money, shame may be felt when we are unable to afford certain things or when we feel like we are not living up to societal standards of financial success. This shame can lead to feelings of inadequacy and low self-worth.

Both guilt and shame can be detrimental to our financial well-being. These negative emotions can lead to avoidance of financial planning and decision-making, as we try to avoid the negative feelings associated with them. This can lead to financial instability and further feelings of guilt and shame.

It is important to recognize and address these negative emotions when they arise. Seeking professional help, such as through therapy or financial coaching, can be beneficial in managing these emotions and improving financial habits. It is also important to remind ourselves that everyone has different financial circumstances and to not compare ourselves to others. By acknowledging and addressing these negative emotions, we can take control of our financial lives and make positive changes for the future.

In conclusion, negative emotions associated with money, such as fear, greed, guilt, and shame, can have a powerful impact on our financial lives. It is important to recognize and address these emotions in order to make sound financial decisions and achieve financial freedom.

3 Positive emotions associated with money: Security, Freedom, Autonomy, Satisfaction

Money is often associated with a range of positive emotions, including security, freedom, autonomy, and satisfaction. These emotions can be experienced by individuals who have a comfortable level of financial stability and are able to afford the things they need and want.

Security is a feeling of safety, protection, and stability. It is the sense that our basic needs will be met and that we have the resources to handle any challenges that may come our way. Money can provide this sense of security in a number of ways.

First and foremost, money can provide financial security. Having a sufficient amount of money allows us to pay our bills, cover our expenses, and have a cushion for emergencies. It allows us to live without the constant worry of financial insecurity, and to plan for the future with confidence.

Money can also provide security in terms of job security. When we have a stable income and a secure job, we can feel confident in our ability to provide for ourselves and our families. This sense of security can lead to greater overall well-being and happiness.

In addition, money can provide security in terms of personal safety. When we have the financial resources to take care of ourselves and our loved ones, we are less vulnerable to harm and less reliant on others for support. This can give us a greater sense of control over our lives and increase our feelings of security.

While money can't buy happiness, it can provide the

foundation for a sense of stability and security that is crucial for our overall well-being and contentment.

One of the most positive emotions associated with money is the feeling of freedom it can bring. When you have financial stability and resources, you have the ability to make choices and decisions about your life without the constraints of financial stress or insecurity.

The freedom that comes with having money can take many forms. For example, if you have enough financial resources, you may be able to afford to take time off work to travel or pursue a personal hobby. This can be a great source of joy and fulfillment, as it allows you to explore your passions and interests without worrying about how you will pay your bills.

Another way in which money can bring freedom is by providing security. When you have a financial cushion, you are less likely to worry about unexpected expenses or emergencies. This can be especially important if you have a family or other dependents, as it allows you to provide for their needs without constantly worrying about how you will meet your financial obligations.

In addition to providing security and the ability to pursue your passions, having financial resources can also give you the freedom to make choices about your career and professional path. For example, you may be able to afford to take a lower paying job that you are more passionate about, or you may have the resources to invest in your own business or start a new venture.

Ultimately, the freedom that comes with having money can allow you to live a more fulfilling and enjoyable life. It can provide a sense of control and autonomy, and allow you to pursue your goals and dreams without the constraints of financial insecurity.

Autonomy is the sense of being in control of your own life, of having the freedom to make your own decisions and choices. It's an important aspect of well-being, and having financial autonomy can contribute significantly to our overall happiness and satisfaction with life.

There are several ways in which financial autonomy can bring positive emotions. First, it can give us a sense of security and stability. When we have financial resources, we feel more confident and secure in our ability to meet our basic needs and take care of ourselves and our families. This sense of security can reduce stress and anxiety, and allow us to focus on other areas of our lives with more peace of mind.

Second, financial autonomy can provide a sense of independence and self-reliance. When we don't have to rely on others for financial support, we feel more self-sufficient and capable of taking care of ourselves. This can boost our confidence and self-esteem, and give us a greater sense of control over our lives.

Finally, financial autonomy can give us the freedom to pursue our dreams and goals. When we have the resources to support ourselves, we can take risks and pursue opportunities that may not be possible without financial security. This can bring a sense of excitement and fulfillment, as we work towards achieving our goals and making our dreams a reality.

Overall, financial autonomy can bring a range of positive emotions, from a sense of security and stability to the freedom to pursue our dreams and goals. While it's important to recognize that money can't buy happiness, it can certainly contribute to our overall sense of well-being and provide us with the resources and freedom to live fulfilling lives.

Satisfaction is a feeling of contentment and fulfillment that comes from achieving a goal or desire. For many people, having a certain amount of money can bring a sense of satisfaction because it allows them to achieve things they may not have been able to without it.

For example, someone who has saved up enough money to buy a house may feel a sense of satisfaction knowing that they have accomplished a major financial goal. Similarly, someone who has been able to pay off their student loans or credit card debt may feel a sense of relief and satisfaction knowing that they are no longer burdened by those debts.

In addition to achieving financial goals, having money can also bring satisfaction through the ability to purchase experiences and material items that bring joy and happiness. For example, someone who has saved up enough money to take a dream vacation may feel a sense of satisfaction knowing that they can finally experience a trip they have been wanting to take for a long time. Similarly, someone who has always wanted to own a particular car or piece of jewelry may feel a sense of satisfaction when they are finally able to afford it.

Overall, money can be a source of positive emotions when it is used to provide financial stability and the freedom to make choices that align with our values and goals.

4 The Hidden Value of Money: Discovering Its True Purpose and Power

Money has long been viewed as a means to an end - a tool to buy goods and services, to achieve status and security, or to advance in one's career. However, there is a hidden value to money that often goes unrecognized. When we understand the true purpose and power of money, we can harness its potential to create positive change in our own lives and in the world.

The true purpose of money is not to accumulate wealth or to buy material possessions, but rather to enable us to live our lives to the fullest and to contribute to the greater good. Money gives us the freedom to pursue our passions, to invest in our education and personal growth, and to support the causes and people that matter to us. It allows us to live our values and make a difference in the world.

However, the pursuit of money for its own sake can often lead to negative consequences. Greed, materialism, and a focus on accumulating wealth can lead to a lack of balance and happiness in our lives. On the other hand, when we use money as a means to achieve our values and contribute to the greater good, it can have a transformative effect on ourselves and those around us.

The power of money lies in its ability to create change. When we use it wisely, it can be a force for good, enabling us to support the causes and people that matter to us, to create positive social and environmental impact, and to invest in the future. By understanding the true purpose and power of money, we can use it as a tool to create a better world for ourselves and those around us.

In conclusion, the hidden value of money lies in its ability to enable us to live our values and contribute to the greater good. By understanding its true purpose and power, we can use it wisely to create positive change in our own lives and in the world.

5 Unraveling the World of Equity Markets

The equity markets, also known as the stock markets, are a vital part of the financial system. They provide a platform for companies to raise capital by selling shares to the public and for investors to buy and sell those shares. The equity markets are constantly evolving, and understanding how they work can be a daunting task for even the most seasoned investors. In this chapter, we will delve into the world of equity markets and unravel some of their mysteries.

First, let's define what we mean by "equity." In the context of the equity markets, equity refers to ownership in a company. When you buy shares of a company's stock, you become an owner of that company and are entitled to a share of its profits and assets. The value of your shares is determined by the performance of the company and the demand for its stock.

There are two main types of equity markets: primary and secondary. The primary market is where companies first issue their stocks to the public. This is often done through an initial public offering (IPO), which is a process that allows companies to raise capital by selling shares to the public for the first time. Companies use the proceeds from the IPO to fund their operations and growth.

The secondary market is where investors buy and sell shares of already-issued stocks. This is done through stock exchanges, such as the New York Stock Exchange (NYSE) or the NASDAQ. These exchanges facilitate the buying and selling of stocks through a centralized marketplace. Investors can buy and sell stocks through brokers, who act as intermediaries between buyers and sellers.

In addition to stock exchanges, there are also alternative

trading systems (ATS) that allow investors to buy and sell stocks without going through a traditional exchange. These include electronic communication networks (ECNs) and dark pools. ECNs are electronic platforms that match buyers and sellers of stocks, while dark pools are private exchanges that allow institutional investors to buy and sell large blocks of stocks without revealing their orders to the public.

Now that we have a basic understanding of the equity markets, let's delve into some of the key concepts that investors need to know. One important concept is market capitalization, which refers to the value of a company's outstanding shares. It is calculated by multiplying the number of a company's outstanding shares by its stock price. Companies with large market capitalizations are often considered more established and stable than those with smaller market caps.

Another important concept is the price-to-earnings (P/E) ratio, which is used to gauge the value of a company's stock. It is calculated by dividing a company's stock price by its earnings per share (EPS). A higher P/E ratio indicates that a company's stock is overvalued, while a lower P/E ratio indicates that it is undervalued.

There are also various types of equity securities, including common stock, preferred stock, and warrants. Common stock is the most common type of equity security and gives shareholders the right to vote at shareholder meetings and receive dividends. Preferred stock is a type of equity security that gives shareholders priority over common stockholders in terms of dividends and the liquidation of assets. Warrants are securities that give the holder the right to buy a specified number of shares at a predetermined price within a certain time period.

Finally, it is important to understand the role of market

trends and economic indicators in the equity markets. Market trends are patterns that emerge over time and can provide insight into the direction of the market. Economic indicators, such as GDP, employment data, and inflation, can also impact the performance of the equity markets.

In conclusion, the equity markets are a complex and constantly evolving landscape. By understanding the key concepts and players in the market, investors can make informed decisions.

6 Identifying Growing Markets

As a trader, it is important to constantly be on the lookout for new and growing markets to invest in. These markets can provide new opportunities for profits and diversification of your portfolio. Here are some tips for identifying growing markets:

As a trader, it is important to constantly be on the lookout for growing markets where you can potentially make a profit. One way to identify these markets is by keeping an eye on economic indicators. These indicators can provide valuable information about the overall health and direction of an economy, and can help traders make informed decisions about where to allocate their resources.

There are various types of economic indicators that traders can use to identify growing markets. Some of the most commonly tracked indicators include GDP (gross domestic product), unemployment rates, inflation rates, and consumer confidence.

GDP is a measure of the overall size of an economy and is typically used as a benchmark for economic growth. If GDP is growing, it can be an indication that the economy is healthy and expanding, which can be a good sign for traders looking to invest in that market.

Unemployment rates are another important economic indicator to keep an eye on. A low unemployment rate typically signifies a strong job market, which can lead to increased consumer spending and overall economic growth.

Inflation rates can also provide valuable information for traders. If inflation rates are high, it can indicate that prices are rising, which could potentially lead to increased consumer demand and economic growth. However, if inflation rates are too high, it can also lead to negative consequences, such as decreased consumer confidence and potential market instability.

Consumer confidence is another important economic indicator that traders should pay attention to. When consumers are confident about their financial situation and the overall state of the economy, they are more likely to spend money, which can lead to increased economic growth. Conversely, if consumer confidence is low, it can indicate that consumers are hesitant to spend money, which can lead to slower economic growth.

As a trader, it is crucial to stay updated on industry trends in order to discover growing markets and potential opportunities for profit. Here are a few reasons why:

Industry trends can indicate potential market growth: By following industry trends, traders can get a sense of which markets are on the rise and which ones may be declining. For example, if a particular industry is experiencing an influx of new technologies or an increase in demand, this may be a sign that the market is growing and could potentially provide profitable trading opportunities.

Industry trends can inform investment decisions: By staying up to date on industry trends, traders can make more informed investment decisions. For instance, if a particular industry is experiencing a surge in demand, it may be wise to invest in companies that operate within that industry. On the other hand, if an industry is experiencing a decline, it may be best to avoid investing in companies within that sector.

Industry trends can help traders stay ahead of the competition: By being aware of industry trends, traders can get a head start on their competition and be better positioned to take advantage of emerging opportunities. For example, if a trader is aware of a new technology that is gaining traction in a particular industry, they can invest in companies that are early adopters of that technology and potentially reap the rewards of being ahead of the curve.

Industry trends can provide valuable insight for long-term planning: By following industry trends, traders can better plan for the long-term future of their investments. For instance, if a particular industry is expected to experience significant growth in the coming years, traders can position themselves to take advantage of that growth by investing in companies within that industry.

Emerging markets are defined as countries that are in the process of rapid economic and social development. These markets offer a number of benefits for traders looking to discover growing markets, including:

Higher Growth Potential: Emerging markets typically have higher growth potential compared to developed markets. This is due to their lower levels of economic development, which means there is more room for growth.

Diversification: Trading in emerging markets can provide diversification to a trader's portfolio. By investing in a variety of markets, traders can reduce the risk of concentrating their investments in a single market or industry.

Higher Returns: Emerging markets can offer higher returns compared to developed markets due to their higher risk. This is due to the fact that there is more uncertainty in emerging markets, which can lead to higher volatility.

Innovation: Emerging markets often have a strong focus on innovation and technology. This can provide traders with the opportunity to invest in companies with cutting-edge products and services.

Demographic Changes: Emerging markets often have a young and rapidly growing population. This can create a demand for goods and services, leading to growth in various industries.

Political and social changes can have a significant impact on markets and the economy. As a trader, it is important to analyze these changes in order to discover potential opportunities for growth and success.

One key reason for analyzing political and social changes is that they can affect the stability and reliability of a market. Political instability or social unrest can lead to market volatility, making it difficult for traders to make informed decisions about their investments. By staying informed about political and social developments, traders can better understand the risks associated with certain markets and make more informed decisions about where to invest their capital.

In addition to providing insight into market stability, analyzing political and social changes can also help traders identify new opportunities for growth. For example, changes in government policies or regulations can create new markets or open up previously restricted sectors. Similarly, social trends and shifting consumer preferences can create demand for new products or services, providing opportunities for traders to enter and profit from these emerging markets.

Furthermore, understanding political and social changes can help traders adapt to changes in the market and adjust their strategies accordingly. For example, if a country experiences political instability, traders may need to consider alternative markets or adjust their risk management strategies to protect their investments. By analyzing and understanding these changes, traders can better position themselves to take advantage of new opportunities or mitigate potential risks.

Monitoring global events is crucial for traders as it allows them to discover growing markets and capitalize on potential opportunities. By keeping an eye on current events and trends, traders can stay ahead of the game and make informed decisions about where to invest their money.

There are several reasons why traders should monitor global events. First, global events can have a significant impact on financial markets. For example, if there is a political crisis in a country, it could lead to economic instability and a decrease in the value of its currency. By monitoring such events, traders can avoid investing in markets that are likely to experience volatility and instead, focus on markets that are more stable and likely to offer better returns.

Second, global events can also provide insight into emerging markets that are on the rise. For example, if there is a new technological innovation in a particular industry, traders can identify which markets are likely to benefit from this development and invest accordingly. By staying up-to-date on global events, traders can identify potential growth opportunities and get in on the ground floor.

Third, monitoring global events can help traders diversify their portfolio. By investing in a variety of markets, traders can reduce their overall risk and increase the chances of achieving consistent returns. By staying informed about global events, traders can identify new markets that are worth exploring and build a diverse portfolio that can weather any market fluctuations.

By keeping an eye on economic indicators, industry trends, emerging markets, political and social changes, and global events, traders can identify growing markets and take advantage of new opportunities for profits.

7 Why You Want to Trade the Markets

There are many reasons why people choose to trade the markets. For some, it is a way to make extra income or supplement their current income. For others, it is a full-time career that allows them to be their own boss and have the freedom to work from anywhere in the world.

One of the main reasons people want to trade the markets is the potential for financial gain. The markets offer endless opportunities to make money, and with the right strategies and risk management, traders can potentially earn significant profits.

Another reason people want to trade the markets is the excitement and thrill it brings. Trading can be a highly stimulating and challenging activity, and the constant changes in the markets can keep traders on their toes.

Traders also have the opportunity to learn and grow as they navigate the markets. Trading requires ongoing learning and development, and traders have the opportunity to continually improve their skills and knowledge.

Additionally, trading can offer a sense of accomplishment and satisfaction. When traders successfully execute a trade and see their profits grow, it can be a feeling of great accomplishment and pride.

Trading the markets allows for a certain level of flexibility in terms of where and when individuals can work. With the ability to trade online, traders can work from anywhere with an internet connection. This can be especially appealing for those who value work-life balance or who want to work on their own terms.

Overall, trading the markets can offer a range of benefits, from financial gain and excitement to learning and personal fulfillment. It is a challenging and rewarding activity that can be highly rewarding for those who are willing to put in the time and effort to succeed.

8 Introduction to the Trader's Mindset

The trader's mindset is a crucial aspect of successful trading. It refers to the way a trader thinks and approaches the markets, and it can have a significant impact on their ability to make informed and profitable decisions. A trader with a strong mindset is able to manage their emotions, maintain discipline, and adhere to their trading plan.

The trader's mindset is not something that can be developed overnight. It takes time and discipline to cultivate a mental approach that is conducive to successful trading. However, it is possible to make progress in this area with the right mindset and determination.

One key aspect of the trader's mindset is the ability to manage emotions. Trading can be an emotionally charged activity, with the potential for large profits and losses. It is essential for traders to be able to control their emotions and not let them interfere with their decision-making process. This can be especially challenging when a trade goes against them, or when they are faced with unexpected market conditions.

To manage emotions effectively, traders must be able to maintain perspective and focus on the long-term goals of their trading strategy. This requires a level of detachment from the markets and a willingness to accept that not every trade will be a winner.

Another important aspect of the trader's mindset is discipline. Trading requires discipline in a number of areas, including adhering to a pre-determined trading plan, maintaining a consistent approach, and avoiding impulsive decisions.

Discipline is also essential in the areas of risk management and money management. Traders must be able to stay within their risk tolerance and follow a plan for managing their capital. This requires discipline in the form of self-control and the ability to stick to a set of rules.

Finally, a key aspect of the trader's mindset is the ability to continuously learn and adapt. The markets are constantly changing, and traders must be able to adapt to new information and market conditions. This requires a willingness to learn and an openness to new ideas.

In conclusion, the trader's mindset is a crucial aspect of successful trading. It involves the ability to manage emotions, maintain discipline, and continuously learn and adapt. While it takes time and discipline to develop, a strong mindset can make a significant difference in a trader's ability to make informed and profitable decisions.

9 How to Generate Wealth by Trading the Markets

Trading the markets can be a lucrative way to generate wealth, but it requires a certain level of knowledge, skill, and discipline. Here are some tips on how to effectively trade the markets and maximize your wealth-building potential.

Before diving into the world of trading, it is crucial to educate oneself on the various aspects of the markets. This includes understanding the different types of financial instruments and their corresponding risks, learning about market trends and analysis techniques, and developing a solid trading strategy.

One of the main reasons to educate oneself before trading is to minimize the risk of financial losses. The markets can be volatile and unpredictable, and without proper knowledge and understanding, traders may make poor investment decisions that result in significant losses. By educating oneself on the various factors that can impact the markets, traders can make more informed decisions and mitigate their risk.

Another reason to educate oneself before trading is to maximize profits. By understanding the various financial instruments and their corresponding risks, traders can make more informed decisions about which instruments to trade and how to best approach them. This can help traders to maximize their profits by selecting the most profitable instruments and implementing effective trading strategies.

In addition to minimizing risk and maximizing profits, educating oneself before trading can also help traders to build confidence in their abilities. When traders have a solid understanding of the markets and trading strategies, they are more likely to approach their trades with confidence and make decisions with conviction. This can lead to better trading results and a more successful overall trading experience.

Developing a trading plan is an essential step for any trader before entering the markets. A trading plan serves as a blueprint for all of your trades, outlining your goals, strategies, risk management techniques, and other important aspects of your trading approach. By having a clear and well-defined plan in place, you can better navigate the markets, manage your risk, and achieve your desired results.

There are several key reasons why it is important to develop a trading plan before trade the markets:

Define your goals and objectives: A trading plan helps you to clearly define your goals and objectives for your trading activity. This includes setting financial targets, such as your desired profit or loss, as well as non-financial goals, such as improving your skills or gaining experience. By knowing exactly what you want to achieve, you can tailor your trading strategies to suit your goals and measure your progress towards meeting them.

Develop a trading strategy: A trading plan outlines the specific strategies that you will use to trade the markets. This includes the types of markets you will trade, the instruments you will use, and the specific tactics you will employ. By having a clear and consistent approach, you can improve your chances of success and reduce the likelihood of making impulsive or emotional decisions.

Manage risk: A trading plan helps you to manage risk by outlining the amount of capital you are willing to risk on each trade and establishing stop-loss orders to minimize potential losses. By having a solid risk management plan in place, you can protect your capital and minimize the impact of potential losses on your overall trading account.

Improve discipline: A trading plan helps you to maintain discipline by forcing you to follow a set of rules and guidelines. This includes following a specific trading schedule, adhering to your risk management rules, and staying focused on your goals and objectives. By sticking to your plan, you can avoid making impulsive or emotional decisions that may jeopardize your success.

Stay on track: A trading plan helps you to stay on track and avoid getting sidetracked by market noise or external distractions. By having a clear plan in place, you can focus on your trades and avoid getting caught up in the hype or emotional turmoil that can sometimes accompany the markets.

Overall, developing a trading plan is an essential step for any trader looking to succeed in the markets. By defining your goals, developing a trading strategy, managing risk, and staying disciplined, you can improve your chances of success and achieve your desired results.

Risk management is an essential part of any successful trading strategy. It is the process of identifying, assessing, and prioritizing potential risks in order to minimize their impact on your trades. By implementing risk management techniques before entering the market, you can protect yourself from unexpected losses and maximize your potential for profits.

There are several reasons why it is important to use risk management techniques before trading the markets.

First and foremost, risk management helps you to identify potential risks and develop strategies to mitigate them. This includes assessing the level of risk associated with a particular trade and determining the appropriate risk-reward ratio. By understanding the potential risks and rewards of a trade, you can make informed decisions about whether or not to enter the market.

Second, risk management helps you to manage your capital more effectively. By setting appropriate risk levels and stop loss orders, you can ensure that your trades are not overly risky and that you are not exposing yourself to unnecessary losses. This can help you to preserve your capital and maintain a healthy trading account.

Third, risk management helps you to be more disciplined in your trading. By following a set of risk management rules, you can avoid the temptation to take on too much risk or enter into trades that are not in line with your overall trading strategy. This can help you to stay focused and avoid costly mistakes.

Finally, risk management can help you to achieve better returns on your trades. By minimizing your risk and maximizing your potential for profits, you can increase your overall returns and build a more successful trading career.

Risk management techniques are essential for any trader looking to succeed in the markets. By implementing risk management strategies before entering the market, you can protect yourself from unexpected losses, manage your capital more effectively, be more disciplined in your trading, and achieve better returns on your trades.

Staying disciplined in the markets is essential for any trader, regardless of their level of experience or trading style. There are several key reasons why traders must stay disciplined in order to be successful in the markets.

First and foremost, discipline helps traders to maintain a clear and focused mindset. The markets can be unpredictable and chaotic at times, and it is easy to get caught up in the hype or fear of a particular trade. However, discipline allows traders to stay calm and focused, even in the face of market volatility or uncertainty. This allows traders to make better informed and more rational decisions, rather than letting their emotions or biases get the better of them.

Discipline also helps traders to stick to their trading plan and strategy. It is easy to get swayed by the opinions of others or to deviate from your original plan when things are not going as expected. However, discipline allows traders to stay true to their plan and follow it consistently, even when things do not go as planned. This can help to prevent impulsive or reckless trades, which can lead to significant losses.

Discipline is also crucial for risk management and money management. By staying disciplined, traders can better control their risk exposure and ensure that they are not overleveraging their positions or taking on too much risk. This can help to prevent costly mistakes and ensure that traders are maximizing their profits and minimizing their losses.

Discipline helps traders to be more consistent and patient in their trading. It allows traders to wait for the right opportunities and be patient for those opportunities to present themselves. This can be especially important in the short-term markets, where traders may need to wait for the right moment to enter or exit a trade. By staying disciplined, traders can avoid making hasty or rash decisions and instead focus on the long-term success of their trading.

In conclusion, discipline is an essential quality for any trader to have in order to be successful in the markets. It helps traders to maintain a clear and focused mindset, stick to their trading plan and strategy, manage their risk and money effectively, and be consistent and patient in their trading. By staying disciplined, traders can increase their chances of success and ultimately achieve their trading goals.

Staying updated on market news and trends is crucial for anyone who is looking to trade the markets. There are several reasons why it is important to stay updated, and some of the most important ones are discussed below.

To make informed decisions: To make informed decisions when trading, it is important to have a good understanding of the underlying factors that may affect the market. This includes economic indicators, geopolitical events, and company news. By staying updated, you can get a better sense of the direction that the market is likely to take and make informed decisions accordingly.

To identify opportunities: Staying updated also helps you identify opportunities in the market. This can include new trends that are emerging, changes in market conditions, or even news about companies that may be undervalued or overvalued. By being aware of these opportunities, you can make informed decisions about when to buy or sell a particular asset.

To minimize risk: Trading involves a certain level of risk, but staying updated can help you minimize this risk. For example, if you are aware of economic indicators that may affect the market, you can adjust your trading strategy accordingly. This can help you minimize your risk and potentially maximize your profits.

To stay competitive: The markets are constantly changing, and staying updated helps you stay competitive. By staying informed, you can stay ahead of the curve and make informed decisions that help you stay ahead of the competition.

To avoid losses: Finally, staying updated helps you avoid losses. By being aware of market trends and news, you can avoid making poor decisions that could result in significant losses.

Staying updated is essential for anyone looking to trade the markets. It helps you make informed decisions, identify opportunities, minimize risk, stay competitive, and avoid losses. Therefore, it is important to regularly read market news and stay informed about the latest trends and developments in the world of trading.

Diversifying your portfolio means spreading your investments across a range of different assets, industries, and geographic regions. The goal of diversification is to reduce the overall risk of your portfolio by ensuring that your investments are not too heavily concentrated in any one particular area. This can be especially important when it comes to trading the markets, as the value of individual assets can be highly volatile and subject to significant fluctuations.

One of the main reasons to diversify your portfolio for trading the markets is to mitigate the risk of loss. By investing in a variety of different assets, you can help to reduce the impact of any negative developments in a particular market or sector. For example, if the value of one of your investments declines significantly, it is likely to have a smaller impact on your overall portfolio if you have diversified your holdings.

Another reason to diversify your portfolio is to take advantage of different market conditions. Different asset classes and sectors tend to perform differently at different times, so by investing in a diverse range of assets, you can potentially capture returns from a variety of different market environments. This can be especially important in times of economic uncertainty, when it is more difficult to predict which assets will perform well.

Additionally, diversifying your portfolio can also help to increase the overall return on your investments. By investing in a variety of different assets, you may be able to capture returns from a number of different sources, which can help to boost the overall performance of your portfolio.

There are several different ways to diversify your portfolio when trading the markets. One common approach is to invest in a range of different asset classes, such as stocks, bonds, commodities, and real estate. Another option is to invest in a variety of different sectors, such as technology, healthcare, and financial services. It is also possible to diversify by investing in assets from different geographic regions, such as the United States, Europe, and Asia.

The best approach to diversification will depend on your individual investment goals, risk tolerance, and time horizon. It is important to carefully consider your options and to seek the advice of a financial professional if you are unsure about which investments are right for you.

Continuous learning and improvement is a crucial aspect of trading the markets. It is essential for traders to constantly strive to improve their skills and knowledge in order to stay ahead of the competition and achieve success in their trades.

One of the main reasons to continuously learn and improve is to stay up-to-date with the latest market trends and changes. The financial markets are constantly evolving, and traders need to be aware of these changes in order to make informed decisions about their trades. This can include staying informed about economic events, market news, and technological advancements that could impact the markets.

Another reason to continuously learn and improve is to avoid making costly mistakes. Trading can be a risky endeavor, and even experienced traders can make mistakes that result in significant losses. By continuously learning and improving, traders can identify and avoid potential pitfalls and make better-informed decisions. This can help traders to minimize their losses and increase their chances of success.

In addition to staying informed and avoiding mistakes, continuous learning and improvement can also help traders to identify and take advantage of new opportunities in the market. By staying up-to-date on the latest market trends and changes, traders can identify potential trade opportunities that they may have missed otherwise. This can be especially useful for traders who are looking to diversify their portfolio and explore new investment opportunities.

Finally, continuous learning and improvement can also help traders to develop their skills and knowledge to the point where they can make trades with greater confidence and accuracy. By constantly learning and improving, traders can become more skilled and knowledgeable about the markets, which can help them to make better-informed trades and increase their chances of success.

There are many compelling reasons for traders to continuously learn and improve. By staying up-to-date on the latest market trends and changes, avoiding mistakes, identifying new opportunities, and developing their skills and knowledge, traders can increase their chances of success and achieve their trading goals.

By following these tips, you can effectively trade the markets and generate wealth over time. However, it's important to keep in mind that trading carries inherent risks, and you should always do your due diligence before making any trades.

10 How Much Money to Start Trading the Markets

When it comes to trading the markets, one of the most common questions that people ask is how much money they need to get started. This is a valid concern, as it is important to ensure that you have sufficient capital to cover your potential losses and to allow you to make a profit.

The amount of money that you need to start trading will depend on a variety of factors, including your experience level, the type of trading you plan to do, and the amount of risk that you are comfortable with. Here are some things to consider when determining how much money you need to start trading the markets.

The amount of money that you should use for trading the markets will depend on your experience level. As a beginner, it is important to start with a small amount of money to get a feel for the markets and to learn how to trade effectively. This will allow you to make mistakes and learn from them without risking too much capital. As you gain more experience and become more comfortable with trading, you can gradually increase the amount of money that you use.

There are several factors that you should consider when deciding how much money to use for trading. One of the most important is your risk tolerance. This refers to your ability to withstand losses and maintain your discipline as a trader. If you are risk-averse, you may want to start with a smaller amount of money to ensure that you do not suffer significant losses. On the other hand, if you are more willing to take on risk, you may be able to start with a larger amount of money.

Another factor to consider is your trading strategy. Different strategies may require different amounts of capital to be effective. For example, a swing trader who holds positions for a few days to a few weeks may need less capital than a day trader who holds positions for a shorter period of time. This is because the day trader may need to cover the costs of more frequent trades, such as commissions and slippage.

Finally, you should consider your overall financial situation when deciding how much money to use for trading. It is important to only use money that you can afford to lose, and to not compromise your financial security or quality of life in order to trade. You should also consider the potential opportunity costs of using money for trading, such as the potential returns that you could earn by investing in other assets.

Trading strategies are essential tools for traders as they allow them to make informed decisions and seek to maximize their profits in the markets. The type of trading strategy that a trader employs can significantly impact the amount of money that they will be operating with.

There are various types of trading strategies that traders can use, and each of them comes with its own set of risks and potential rewards. Some strategies, such as day trading, require a large amount of capital to be effective, as they involve making numerous trades in a single day and require the trader to have enough capital to cover the potential losses from these trades.

On the other hand, some strategies, such as swing trading or position trading, involve holding onto trades for a longer period of time and may not require as much capital upfront. These strategies may be more suitable for traders with smaller accounts or those who are looking to trade with a more conservative approach.

It is essential for traders to carefully consider the type of trading strategy they will be employing and how it aligns with their financial goals and risk tolerance. If a trader is not adequately capitalized for the type of strategy they are using, they may be at a higher risk of losing their entire trading account.

The type of trading strategy that a trader uses can significantly impact the amount of money they will be operating with in the markets. It is crucial for traders to carefully consider their strategies and ensure that they have the appropriate amount of capital to support their trades.

Risk tolerance is an essential factor that traders must consider when determining the amount of money they will be operating with in the markets. Risk tolerance refers to a person's willingness to take on risk in pursuit of potential returns and can vary significantly from one individual to another.

Traders with a high risk tolerance may be more comfortable operating with a larger amount of capital, as they are willing to accept the possibility of higher losses in exchange for the potential for larger returns. These traders may be more inclined towards strategies that involve a higher level of risk, such as day trading or high-leverage trading.

On the other hand, traders with a low risk tolerance may be more comfortable operating with a smaller amount of capital and may prefer strategies that involve a lower level of risk. These traders may be more inclined towards strategies such as swing trading or position trading, which involve holding onto trades for a longer period of time and may not require as much capital upfront.

It is essential for traders to assess their risk tolerance and ensure that they are comfortable with the level of risk they are taking on with their trades. Trading with an amount of capital that exceeds their risk tolerance can lead to significant losses and may even result in the loss of their entire trading account.

Risk tolerance is a critical factor that can impact the amount of money with which traders operate in the markets. Traders should carefully consider their risk tolerance and ensure that their trading capital aligns with their level of risk tolerance and their financial goals.

The costs of commissions when trading can significantly impact the amount of money with which traders will operate in the markets. Commission costs are fees that are charged by brokers for facilitating trades on behalf of their clients. These costs can vary significantly depending on the broker and the type of asset being traded.

For traders who are operating with a small amount of capital, the costs of commissions can eat into their profits and may even result in losses. As a result, these traders may choose to limit the number of trades they make or opt for brokers that offer lower commission costs.

On the other hand, traders operating with a larger amount of capital may have more flexibility in terms of the number of trades they can make and may be able to absorb the costs of commissions more easily. These traders may also be able to negotiate lower commission costs with their brokers due to the larger volume of trades they are making.

It is essential for traders to consider the costs of commissions when determining the amount of money they will be operating with in the markets. By carefully evaluating their trading capital and the costs of commissions, traders can better align their trading activities with their financial goals and minimize the impact of these costs on their profits.

The costs of commissions can significantly impact the amount of money with which traders operate in the markets. Traders should carefully consider these costs and align their trading capital and strategies accordingly to maximize their profits and minimize losses.

In general, it is recommended to start with at least $500 to $1,000 if you are planning on day trading, and at least $5,000 to $10,000 if you are planning on long-term trading. These amounts will provide you with sufficient capital to cover your costs and to allow you to make a profit.

However, it is important to keep in mind that these are just rough estimates, and the amount of capital you need to start trading may vary depending on your individual circumstances. It is always a good idea to consult with a financial advisor or professional trader before making any investment decisions.

11 How to Control Risk When Trading Markets

Controlling risk when trading the markets is an essential aspect of successful trading. In this chapter, we will delve deeper into various techniques that traders can use to control risk when trading the markets.

Use risk management tools: Stop-loss orders and take-profit orders are essential tools for controlling risk when trading. A stop-loss order is an instruction to close a trade when the market moves against the trader by a certain amount, while a take-profit order is an instruction to close a trade when the market moves in favor of the trader by a certain amount. These orders can help traders minimize losses and lock in profits.
For example, let's say a trader buys 100 shares of XYZ company at $50 per share. If the trader sets a stop-loss order at $45, the trade will be automatically closed if the price of XYZ falls to $45 or lower, limiting the trader's loss to $500 (100 shares x $5 loss per share). Similarly, if the trader sets a take-profit order at $55, the trade will be automatically closed if the price of XYZ rises to $55 or higher, locking in a profit of $500 (100 shares x $5 profit per share).

In addition to stop-loss and take-profit orders, traders can also use other risk management tools such as trailing stop-loss orders and limit orders. A trailing stop-loss order adjusts the stop-loss level as the market moves in favor of the trader, while a limit order allows the trader to set a maximum price they are willing to pay for a security or a minimum price at which they are willing to sell.

Manage position size: Position size is the amount of a particular asset that a trader owns. By carefully managing position size, traders can ensure that a single trade does not have the potential to significantly impact their overall account balance. This can be achieved by using risk management techniques such as the 1% rule, which states that the maximum risk on any single trade should be no more than 1% of the trader's account balance.

For example, if a trader has a $50,000 account balance and they want to follow the 1% rule, their maximum risk on any single trade should be no more than $500 (1% of $50,000). If the trader is trading a security with a price of $100 per share, they should not buy more than 5 shares (500 / 100 = 5) to stay within the 1% risk limit.

In addition to the 1% rule, traders can also use other position sizing techniques such as the fixed fractional method, which involves setting a fixed percentage of the account balance that will be allocated to each trade.

Diversify your portfolio: Diversification involves spreading investments across a variety of different asset classes, such as stocks, bonds, and commodities. By diversifying, traders can reduce the overall risk of their portfolio.

For example, if a trader has a portfolio consisting solely of tech stocks, they are taking on a significant amount of sector-specific risk. If the tech sector were to experience a downturn, the trader's portfolio would likely suffer as a result. On the other hand, if the trader diversifies their portfolio to include a mix of stocks from different sectors, such as tech, healthcare, and financials, they are spreading out their risk across multiple sectors and are less likely to be adversely impacted by a downturn in any single sector.

In addition to diversifying across asset classes, traders can also diversify within asset classes. For example, a trader who is interested in the stock market can diversify their portfolio by investing in a mix of large cap, mid cap, and small cap stocks. This can help reduce the overall risk of the portfolio by reducing the impact of any single stock or sector on the portfolio's performance.

Consider the risk-reward ratio: The risk-reward ratio is a measure of the potential return of a trade relative to the amount of risk taken. Trades with a favorable risk-reward ratio have a higher probability of success and should be given preference.

For example, if a trader is considering a trade with a potential reward of $500 and a potential risk of $100, the risk-reward ratio is 5:1 (500 / 100 = 5). This means that for every $1 of risk, the trader has the potential to earn $5 in return. A risk-reward ratio of 5:1 is generally considered to be favorable, as it indicates that the potential reward is significantly greater than the risk taken.

Traders can use the risk-reward ratio to determine the appropriate position size for a trade. For example, if a trader has a $50,000 account balance and they want to follow the 1% rule, their maximum risk on any single trade should be no more than $500 (1% of $50,000). If the trader is considering a trade with a risk-reward ratio of 5:1 and a potential risk of $500, the potential reward of the trade would be $2,500 (500 x 5). This would allow the trader to allocate a position size of 25 shares (2,500 / 100 = 25) to the trade while still staying within the 1% risk limit.

Have a trading plan: A comprehensive trading plan can help traders stay disciplined and make informed decisions based on their risk tolerance and investment goals. A trading plan should outline the trader's risk management strategies as well as their entry and exit criteria for trades.

A trading plan should include the following elements:

Risk management strategies: This should include the use of risk management tools such as stop-loss and take-profit orders, as well as the trader's position sizing strategy.

Entry criteria: This should outline the specific conditions that need to be met in order for the trader to enter a trade, such as a breakout of a key technical level or a fundamental trigger.

Exit criteria: This should outline the specific conditions that will cause the trader to exit a trade, such as a breach of a key support or resistance level or a change in market conditions.

By following a well-defined trading plan, traders can stay disciplined and make informed, risk-controlled trades.

In conclusion, controlling risk when trading the markets is an essential aspect of successful trading. By using risk management tools, managing position size, diversifying their portfolio, considering the risk-reward ratio, and having a comprehensive trading plan, traders can effectively control risk and increase the chances of success in the markets.

It is important for traders to regularly review and adjust their risk management strategies as needed. Markets are constantly changing and traders should be prepared to adapt to these changes in order to stay ahead of the game.

One way traders can do this is by regularly reviewing their portfolio to ensure that it is properly diversified. If a particular asset class or sector begins to make up a disproportionate amount of the portfolio, traders may want to consider reallocating some of their investments to other asset classes or sectors in order to maintain a balanced portfolio.

Traders should also regularly review their risk management tools to ensure that they are appropriate for the current market environment. For example, if a trader is using a fixed stop-loss order and the market becomes more volatile, they may want to consider adjusting their stop-loss order to a trailing stop-loss in order to allow for more flexibility.

It is also important for traders to review their trading plan on a regular basis. As traders gain more experience, they may find that their risk tolerance or investment goals have changed, and their trading plan should reflect these changes.

In addition to regular review and adjustment, traders should also be prepared for unexpected events that can impact the markets. This includes staying up to date on economic and geopolitical news that may affect the markets, as well as having a plan in place for handling market disruptions such as flash crashes or prolonged periods of volatility.

By regularly reviewing and adjusting their risk management strategies and being prepared for unexpected events, traders can effectively control risk and increase the chances of success in the markets.

It is also important for traders to have a solid understanding of risk and how it affects their trades. This includes understanding the types of risk that can impact trades, such as market risk, credit risk, and liquidity risk.

Market risk refers to the risk of loss due to changes in the market value of an asset. For example, if a trader buys a stock and the price of the stock falls, the trader will experience a loss. Market risk is inherent in all trades and cannot be completely eliminated.

Credit risk refers to the risk of loss due to the inability of a counterparty to fulfill their obligations. This can be a concern when trading derivatives such as futures or options, as the trader is relying on the counterparty to fulfill their end of the contract.

Liquidity risk refers to the risk of loss due to an inability to quickly buy or sell an asset. This can be a concern in thin markets or when trading illiquid assets.

By understanding the types of risk that can impact their trades, traders can make informed decisions about the level of risk they are willing to take on and implement appropriate risk management strategies.

In addition to understanding risk, it is also important for traders to have a clear understanding of their own risk tolerance. Different traders have different levels of risk tolerance, and it is important for traders to know their own limits in order to make informed decisions about the level of risk they are comfortable taking on.

Traders can determine their risk tolerance through a variety of methods, such as by assessing their financial goals and resources, their investment horizon, and their overall comfort level with risk. By understanding their own risk tolerance, traders can make informed decisions about the level of risk they are willing to take on and develop a trading plan that aligns with their risk tolerance.

In conclusion, controlling risk when trading the markets is an essential aspect of successful trading. By using risk management tools, managing position size, diversifying their portfolio, considering the risk-reward ratio, and having a comprehensive trading plan, traders can effectively control risk and increase the chances of success in the markets. It is also important for traders to have a solid understanding of risk and their own risk tolerance, and to regularly review and adjust their risk management strategies as needed. By doing so, traders can stay ahead of the game and navigate the markets with confidence.

12 WHAT QUALITIES DO YOU NEED TO OPERATE THE MARKETS?

Operating in the financial markets requires a combination of both technical and personal skills. Here are some qualities that can be useful for someone looking to succeed in the markets:

Knowledge: It is essential to have a strong understanding of financial concepts, such as economics, accounting, and market trends. This includes understanding financial instruments, such as stocks, bonds, and derivatives, as well as the principles of risk management.

Numeracy: The ability to understand and work with numerical data is crucial in the financial markets. This includes being able to analyze and interpret financial statements, as well as being able to perform calculations and make informed decisions based on numerical data.

Analytical skills: The ability to think critically and analyze data is essential in the financial markets. This includes being able to identify trends and patterns, as well as being able to make informed predictions about future market movements.

Attention to detail: The financial markets involve a large amount of data and it is important to be able to pay attention to detail and accurately analyze and interpret this information.

Communication skills: The ability to effectively communicate with clients, colleagues, and other stakeholders is essential in the financial markets. This includes being able to present data and ideas clearly and concisely, as well as being able to listen and understand the needs and concerns of others.

Decision-making: Operating in the financial markets often involves making rapid decisions based on incomplete information. It is important to be able to weigh the potential risks and rewards of different options and make well-informed decisions.

Resilience: The financial markets can be volatile and it is important to be able to handle stress and setbacks. This includes being able to maintain a positive attitude and remain focused in the face of adversity.

Adaptability: The financial markets are constantly changing and it is important to be able to adapt to new situations and information. This includes being open to learning and willing to change strategies as needed.

Integrity: Building and maintaining trust is essential in the financial markets. This includes being honest and transparent in all interactions and acting in the best interests of clients and stakeholders.

Overall, operating in the financial markets requires a combination of technical knowledge, analytical skills, attention to detail, and personal qualities such as resilience and integrity. By cultivating these qualities, individuals can increase their chances of success in the markets.

Discipline is a key quality for a trader to possess. Trading requires the ability to follow a set of rules and stick to a plan, even in the face of temptation or uncertainty. This includes discipline in managing risk, as well as discipline in adhering to a trading strategy.

Patience is also important for a trader. It is not uncommon for trades to take time to play out and it is important to be able to wait for the right opportunities to present themselves. This can help traders avoid making impulsive decisions that may not align with their long-term goals.

Self-confidence is essential for a trader to have in order to make decisive trades. This includes the confidence to enter and exit trades, as well as the confidence to stick to a plan even when faced with challenges.

Objectivity is important for a trader to maintain in order to make unbiased decisions. It is important to be able to separate personal emotions from trading decisions and to base trades on facts and data rather than subjective opinions.

Adaptability is also important for a trader to possess in order to be able to adjust to changing market conditions. This includes the ability to adapt to new information and to alter a trading strategy as needed in response to changing circumstances.

Overall, discipline, patience, self-confidence, objectivity, and adaptability are all important qualities for a trader to possess. By cultivating these qualities, traders can increase their chances of success in the markets.

13 THE IMPORTANCE OF DISCIPLINE IN TRADING

Discipline is a crucial quality for a trader to possess. It requires the ability to follow a set of rules and stick to a plan, even in the face of temptation or uncertainty. This includes discipline in managing risk, as well as discipline in adhering to a trading strategy.

One aspect of discipline in trading is the ability to follow a risk management plan. This involves setting clear guidelines for how much capital to allocate to each trade and how much overall risk to take on. It also involves setting stop-loss orders to minimize potential losses. By following a disciplined risk management plan, traders can avoid taking on excessive risk and can protect their capital from large losses.

Another aspect of discipline in trading is the ability to stick to a trading strategy. This involves developing a plan for when to enter and exit trades, as well as identifying key technical or fundamental indicators to guide decision-making. It is important for traders to have discipline in following their strategy and not deviating from it based on emotions or external influences.

In addition to discipline in managing risk and adhering to a trading strategy, it is also important for traders to be disciplined in their overall approach to the markets. This includes being consistent in their analysis and decision-making, as well as maintaining a clear head and not letting emotions cloud judgment.

Overall, discipline is essential for a trader to succeed in the markets. It requires the ability to follow a plan, manage risk effectively, and stay focused and objective in the face of challenges. By cultivating discipline, traders can increase their chances of success and minimize potential losses.

14 PATIENCE AS THE KEY TO SUCCESS IN THE MARKETS

Patience is an important quality for a trader to possess. It is not uncommon for trades to take time to play out and it is important to be able to wait for the right opportunities to present themselves. This can help traders avoid making impulsive decisions that may not align with their long-term goals.

One aspect of patience in trading is the ability to wait for the right entry points. This may involve waiting for a specific technical or fundamental indicator to be met before entering a trade. It may also involve waiting for market conditions to become more favorable before taking action. By being patient and waiting for the right opportunities, traders can increase their chances of success and minimize potential losses.

Another aspect of patience in trading is the ability to hold onto a trade for the right amount of time. This may involve holding onto a trade until a specific price target is met, or until a key technical or fundamental indicator is reached. It is important for traders to have patience in holding onto trades and not to panic and exit too early.

In addition to patience in entering and exiting trades, it is also important for traders to be patient in their overall approach to the markets. This includes being willing to wait for the right opportunities and not trying to force trades that may not be favorable. It also involves being patient in the face of short-term setbacks and not getting discouraged by temporary setbacks.

Overall, patience is essential for a trader to succeed in the markets. It requires the ability to wait for the right opportunities, hold onto trades for the right amount of time, and maintain a long-term perspective. By cultivating patience, traders can increase their chances of success and minimize potential losses.

15 SELF-CONFIDENCE AND TRADING TOOLS

Self-confidence is an essential quality for a trader to possess. It involves the belief in one's abilities and the ability to make decisive trades. This includes the confidence to enter and exit trades, as well as the confidence to stick to a plan even when faced with challenges.

One aspect of self-confidence in trading is the ability to make decisions and take action. This may involve making rapid decisions based on incomplete information, such as entering or exiting a trade in response to a news event or market signal. It is important for traders to have self-confidence in their ability to make decisions and to not second-guess themselves or hesitate when action is needed.

Another aspect of self-confidence in trading is the ability to stick to a plan. This involves developing a trading strategy and having the confidence to follow it even in the face of adversity. It is important for traders to have self-confidence in their strategy and not to abandon it too quickly in the face of setbacks or unexpected market movements.

In addition to confidence in decision-making and sticking to a plan, it is also important for traders to have self-confidence in their overall approach to the markets. This includes believing in one's abilities to analyze and interpret market data, as well as having confidence in one's ability to adapt to new information and changing market conditions.

Overall, self-confidence is essential for a trader to succeed in the markets. It involves believing in one's abilities, being decisive, and having the confidence to stick to a plan. By cultivating self-confidence, traders can increase their chances of success and minimize potential losses.

16 Objectivity as an Essential Element in Trading Decision Making

Objectivity is an important quality for a trader to possess in order to make unbiased decisions. It involves the ability to separate personal emotions from trading decisions and to base trades on facts and data rather than subjective opinions.

One aspect of objectivity in trading is the ability to remain calm and level-headed, even in the face of market volatility or personal setbacks. This involves avoiding letting emotions, such as greed or fear, cloud judgment and instead making decisions based on a clear analysis of market data.

Another aspect of objectivity in trading is the ability to keep an open mind and consider multiple viewpoints. This may involve seeking out different sources of information and being willing to challenge one's own assumptions and biases. By maintaining objectivity, traders can increase the chances of making well-informed decisions.

In addition to maintaining emotional detachment and an open mind, it is also important for traders to be objective in their overall approach to the markets. This includes being willing to change course if a strategy is not working, rather than stubbornly sticking to an incorrect idea.

Overall, objectivity is essential for a trader to succeed in the markets. It involves being able to separate personal emotions from decision-making, keeping an open mind, and being willing to change course if needed. By cultivating objectivity, traders can increase their chances of success and minimize potential losses.

17 THE IMPORTANCE OF ADAPTABILITY IN A CHANGING MARKET

Adaptability is an important quality for a trader to possess in order to be able to adjust to changing market conditions. This includes the ability to adapt to new information and to alter a trading strategy as needed in response to changing circumstances.

One aspect of adaptability in trading is the ability to continuously learn and stay up-to-date with market developments. This may involve regularly reviewing market data and staying informed about economic and political events that can impact the markets. By being adaptable and open to learning, traders can increase their chances of success in a constantly changing market environment.

Another aspect of adaptability in trading is the ability to adjust a trading strategy as needed. This may involve making changes to a strategy based on new information or market conditions, or adopting a new strategy altogether if the current one is no longer effective. By being adaptable and willing to change course, traders can increase their chances of success and minimize potential losses.

In addition to continuously learning and adjusting a trading strategy, it is also important for traders to be adaptable in their overall approach to the markets. This includes being open to trying new approaches and techniques, as well as being willing to reassess and adjust goals as needed.

Overall, adaptability is essential for a trader to succeed in the markets. It involves being open to learning, being willing to change course, and being flexible in one's approach. By cultivating adaptability, traders can increase their chances of success and minimize potential losses.

18 Emotions in Trading: How to Manage Them for Success

Emotions can play a significant role in trading and it is important to be able to manage them effectively in order to make well-informed decisions. Here are some tips for managing emotions in trading:

Recognizing the role of emotions in trading:
It is important for traders to recognize that emotions are a natural part of the trading process and to be aware of how they can impact decision-making. This includes understanding how emotions such as fear, greed, and hope can influence trades and being conscious of the role they play.

For example, fear of losing money can cause traders to exit a trade too early, even if the trade has the potential to be profitable. Similarly, greed can lead to taking on excessive risk in search of quick profits, which can result in overtrading or making impulsive decisions. By recognizing the role of emotions, traders can become more aware of how they may be affecting their decision-making and take steps to mitigate their impact.

Developing a trading plan:
Having a clear trading plan can help to reduce the impact of emotions on decision-making. This may include setting specific rules for when to enter and exit trades, as well as identifying key technical or fundamental indicators to guide decision-making. By having a plan in place, traders can make more objective decisions and avoid letting emotions dictate their actions.

It is also important for traders to have a long-term

perspective and not get too caught up in short-term market movements. This can help to reduce the emotional impact of trading and enable traders to make more rational decisions. Having a clear understanding of one's financial goals and risk tolerance can also help to inform a trading plan and guide decision-making.

Practicing risk management:
Managing risk effectively can help to reduce the emotional impact of trading. This may include setting stop-loss orders to minimize potential losses and ensuring that the amount of capital at risk is within acceptable limits. By managing risk effectively, traders can feel more in control and be less prone to emotional decision-making. It is also important to diversify investments and not have all eggs in one basket, as this can help to reduce the overall level of risk.

Effective risk management also involves having a solid understanding of one's own risk tolerance and being realistic about the potential risks and rewards of a trade. This may involve setting clear guidelines for how much capital to allocate to each trade and not overleveraging or taking on too much risk. By practicing risk management, traders can increase their chances of success and minimize potential losses.

Taking breaks:
It is important for traders to take breaks and step away from the markets periodically in order to avoid getting overwhelmed by emotions. This may involve setting specific times to review trades or simply taking some time to relax and clear the mind. By taking breaks and recharging, traders can approach the markets with a clearer head and make more objective decisions.

It is also important to maintain a healthy work-life balance and not become too consumed by trading. This may involve setting boundaries around trading activity and making time for other activities and interests outside of the markets. By taking care of one's overall well-being, traders can be better equipped to handle the emotional demands of trading.

Seeking support:
Trading can be a solitary pursuit and it is important to have a support system in place. This may include seeking out a mentor or joining a trading community to share experiences and insights. By having a support system, traders can feel less isolated and be better able to manage their emotions.

It can also be helpful to talk to a therapist or other mental health professional to help process and manage emotions related to trading. This may involve exploring ways to cope with the stress and uncertainty of the markets and developing strategies for managing emotions in a healthy way. By seeking support, traders can increase their chances of success and better navigate the emotional challenges of trading.

Staying informed and continuously learning:
Staying informed and continuously learning is an important aspect of managing emotions in trading. By regularly reviewing market data and staying up-to-date with economic and political events that can impact the markets, traders can feel more in control and be better equipped to make informed decisions.

Continuous learning also involves being open to new ideas and approaches and being willing to adapt to changing market conditions. By staying informed and continuously learning, traders can increase their chances of success and minimize the impact of emotions on decision-making.

Setting realistic expectations:
Setting realistic expectations can help to reduce the emotional impact of trading. This may involve acknowledging

that there will be ups and downs in the markets and that not every trade will be a winner. By having a realistic understanding of the potential risks and rewards of trading, traders can be better prepared for the emotional challenges that may arise.

It is also important for traders to set realistic financial goals and to be patient in working towards them. This may involve building up a track record of consistent profits over time, rather than expecting immediate or outsized returns. By setting realistic expectations, traders can increase their chances of success and better manage their emotions.

Maintaining perspective:
Maintaining perspective is an important aspect of managing emotions in trading. This may involve taking a long-term view and not getting too caught up in short-term market movements. By maintaining perspective, traders can better manage their emotions and make more rational decisions.

It is also important for traders to remember that trading is just one aspect of their overall financial plan and to not let it consume their entire focus. By maintaining a healthy balance between trading and other financial goals and priorities, traders can better manage their emotions and make more informed decisions.

Seeking professional help:
If emotions are becoming overwhelming or negatively impacting trading performance, it may be helpful to seek professional help. This may involve talking to a therapist or other mental health professional to work through any underlying issues or to develop strategies for managing emotions in a healthy way.

In addition to seeking help with personal emotional

issues, traders may also benefit from working with a financial advisor or coach to help develop a trading plan and provide guidance and support. By seeking professional help, traders can increase their chances of success and better navigate the emotional challenges of trading.

Recognizing the importance of self-care:
Self-care is an important aspect of managing emotions in trading. This may involve taking breaks and making time for relaxation and leisure activities, as well as engaging in physical exercise and maintaining a healthy diet. By taking care of one's overall well-being, traders can be better equipped to handle the emotional demands of trading.

It is also important for traders to prioritize their overall well-being and not let trading consume their entire focus. This may involve setting boundaries around trading activity and making time for other activities and interests outside of the markets. By recognizing the importance of self-care, traders can better manage their emotions and increase their chances of success.

In conclusion, managing emotions is an essential part of trading. By recognizing the role of emotions, developing a trading plan, practicing risk management, taking breaks, seeking support, staying informed and continuously learning, setting realistic expectations, maintaining perspective, seeking professional help, and prioritizing self-care, traders can increase their chances of success and make more objective decisions. It is also important to recognize that it is normal to experience a range of emotions in trading and to work on developing strategies for managing them effectively. By cultivating emotional intelligence and developing healthy coping strategies, traders can better navigate the emotional challenges of the markets and increase their chances of long-term success.

19 Developing a Long-Term Mindset in Trading

Developing a long-term mindset in trading can help traders to stay focused on their goals and avoid getting caught up in short-term market movements. Here are some tips for developing a long-term mindset in trading:

Setting clear financial goals:
Having a clear understanding of one's financial goals is an important first step in developing a long-term mindset in trading. This may involve setting specific targets for return on investment, such as a certain percentage of profit per year, or building up a track record of consistent profits over time. It is important for traders to be realistic about the potential risks and rewards of trading and to not expect immediate or outsized returns.

By setting clear financial goals, traders can stay focused on the long-term and avoid getting caught up in short-term market movements. It is also important for traders to review their goals periodically and to make adjustments as necessary based on changing market conditions and personal circumstances. By setting clear financial goals, traders can increase their chances of long-term success and better navigate the challenges of the markets.

Diversifying investments:
Diversifying investments is an important strategy for reducing risk and promoting a long-term perspective. This may involve investing in a variety of asset classes, such as stocks, bonds, and real estate, rather than focusing on a single market or security. By diversifying investments, traders can minimize the impact of short-term market fluctuations and increase the chances of long-term success.

It is also important for traders to consider the level of risk associated with different investment options and to allocate capital accordingly. This may involve conducting thorough research and consulting with a financial advisor or other professional to determine the most appropriate investment mix. By diversifying investments, traders can better manage risk and increase the chances of long-term success.

Staying informed and continuously learning:
Staying informed and continuously learning is an important aspect of developing a long-term mindset in trading. This may involve regularly reviewing market data and staying up-to-date with economic and political events that can impact the markets. By staying informed and continuously learning, traders can increase their chances of success and better navigate the long-term dynamics of the markets.

It is also important for traders to be open to new ideas and approaches and to be willing to adapt to changing market conditions. This may involve seeking out new sources of information, such as industry publications or online courses, or joining a trading community to share experiences and insights. By staying informed and continuously learning, traders can increase their chances of long-term success and better navigate the challenges of the markets.

Practicing risk management:
Effective risk management is an essential part of developing a long-term mindset in trading. This may involve setting stop-loss orders to minimize potential losses and ensuring that the amount of capital at risk is within acceptable limits. By practicing risk management, traders can increase the chances of long-term success and minimize the impact of short-term market fluctuations.

It is also important for traders to have a solid understanding of their own risk tolerance and to be realistic about the potential risks and rewards of a trade. This may involve setting clear guidelines for how much capital to allocate to each trade and not overleveraging or taking on too much risk. By practicing risk management, traders can better manage risk and increase the chances of long-term success.

Staying patient:
Patience is an important quality for traders to cultivate in order to develop a long-term mindset. This may involve being willing to wait for the right opportunities to arise and not getting too caught up in short-term market movements. By staying patient, traders can increase the chances of long-term success and avoid making impulsive decisions.

It is also important for traders to recognize that there will be ups and downs in the markets and to not get too discouraged by short-term setbacks. By staying patient and maintaining a long-term perspective, traders can better navigate the challenges of the markets and increase the chances of success.

Maintaining a long-term perspective:
Maintaining a long-term perspective is an important aspect of developing a long-term mindset in trading. This may involve setting specific time frames for trades, such as holding positions for several months or years, rather than focusing on short-term market movements. By maintaining a long-term perspective, traders can better manage their emotions and avoid getting caught up in short-term fluctuations.

It is also important for traders to have a clear understanding of their financial goals and to stay focused on achieving them. This may involve regularly reviewing progress and making adjustments as necessary based on changing market conditions and personal circumstances. By maintaining a long-term perspective, traders can increase their chances of success and better navigate the challenges of the markets.

Cultivating discipline:
Discipline is an important quality for traders to cultivate in order to develop a long-term mindset. This may involve sticking to a trading plan and not letting emotions dictate decision-making. By cultivating discipline, traders can increase the chances of long-term success and avoid making impulsive decisions.

It is also important for traders to set specific rules for when to enter and exit trades and to follow them consistently. This may involve identifying key technical or fundamental indicators to guide decision-making and not deviating from the plan. By cultivating discipline, traders can better manage their emotions and increase the chances of long-term success.

Maintaining a healthy work-life balance:
Maintaining a healthy work-life balance is an important aspect of developing a long-term mindset in trading. This may involve setting boundaries around trading activity and making time for other activities and interests outside of the markets. By maintaining a healthy balance between trading and other financial goals and priorities, traders can better manage their emotions and increase the chances of long-term success.

It is also important for traders to prioritize their overall well-being and not let trading consume their entire focus. This may involve engaging in physical exercise, maintaining a healthy diet, and taking breaks to relax and recharge. By maintaining a healthy work-life balance, traders can better manage their emotions and increase the chances of long-term success.

Seeking support:
Seeking support is an important aspect of developing a long-term mindset in trading. This may involve seeking out a mentor or joining a trading community to share experiences and insights. By having a support system, traders can feel less isolated and be better able to manage their emotions.

It can also be helpful to talk to a therapist or other mental health professional to help process and manage emotions related to trading. This may involve exploring ways to cope with the stress and uncertainty of the markets and developing strategies for managing emotions in a healthy way. By seeking support, traders can increase their chances of long-term success and better navigate the challenges of the markets.

Recognizing the importance of self-care:
Self-care is an important aspect of developing a long-term mindset in trading. This may involve taking breaks and making time for relaxation and leisure activities, as well as engaging in physical exercise and maintaining a healthy diet. By taking care of one's overall well-being, traders can be better equipped to handle the emotional demands of trading and maintain a long-term perspective.

It is also important for traders to prioritize their overall well-being and not let trading consume their entire focus. This may involve setting boundaries around trading activity and making time for other activities and interests outside of the markets. By recognizing the importance of self-care, traders can better manage their emotions and increase the chances of long-term success.

Fostering resilience:
Fostering resilience is an important aspect of developing a long-term mindset in trading. This may involve developing

strategies for coping with setbacks and maintaining a positive attitude even in the face of challenges. By fostering resilience, traders can increase their chances of long-term success and better navigate the ups and downs of the markets.

It is also important for traders to recognize that there will be ups and downs in the markets and to not get too discouraged by short-term setbacks. By maintaining a long-term perspective and staying focused on their financial goals, traders can better manage their emotions and increase the chances of success.

Cultivating emotional intelligence:
Cultivating emotional intelligence is an important aspect of developing a long-term mindset in trading. This may involve recognizing the role of emotions in decision-making and learning to manage them effectively. By cultivating emotional intelligence, traders can increase their chances of long-term success and better navigate the emotional challenges of the markets.

It is also important for traders to recognize the normalcy of experiencing a range of emotions in trading and to develop healthy coping strategies. This may involve seeking support, engaging in self-care, and working with a therapist or other mental health professional to address any underlying issues. By cultivating emotional intelligence, traders can increase their chances of long-term success and better navigate the challenges of the markets.

Managing stress:
Managing stress is an important aspect of developing a long-term mindset in trading. This may involve developing strategies for coping with the demands of the markets and maintaining a healthy work-life balance. By managing stress, traders can increase their chances of long-term success and better navigate the emotional challenges of trading.

It is also important for traders to recognize the normalcy of experiencing stress in the markets and to seek support when needed. This may involve talking to a therapist or other mental health professional, engaging in self-care, or seeking support from friends and family. By managing stress, traders can increase their chances of long-term success and better navigate the challenges of the markets.

Developing a growth mindset:
Developing a growth mindset is an important aspect of developing a long-term mindset in trading. This may involve viewing setbacks as opportunities for learning and growth rather than as failures. By developing a growth mindset, traders can increase their chances of long-term success and better navigate the challenges of the markets.

It is also important for traders to recognize that learning and growth are ongoing processes and to be open to new ideas and approaches. This may involve seeking out new sources of information, such as industry publications or online courses, or joining a trading community to share experiences and insights. By developing a growth mindset, traders can increase their chances of long-term success and better navigate the challenges of the markets.

Maintaining a positive attitude:
Maintaining a positive attitude is an important aspect of developing a long-term mindset in trading. This may involve finding ways to stay motivated and focused on one's financial goals even in the face of challenges. By maintaining a positive attitude, traders can increase their chances of long-term success and better navigate the emotional challenges of the markets.

It is also important for traders to recognize that there will be ups and downs in the markets and to not let negative emotions consume their focus. This may involve finding ways to stay positive and motivated, such as setting small goals or finding ways to celebrate successes along the way. By maintaining a positive attitude, traders can increase their chances of long-term success and better navigate the challenges of the markets.

Overall, developing a long-term mindset in trading involves setting clear financial goals, diversifying investments, staying informed and continuously learning, practicing risk management, staying patient, maintaining a long-term perspective, cultivating discipline, maintaining a healthy work-life balance, seeking support, recognizing the importance of self-care, fostering resilience, cultivating emotional intelligence, managing stress, developing a growth mindset, and maintaining a positive attitude. By cultivating these qualities, traders can increase their chances of long-term success and better navigate the emotional challenges of trading. It is also important for traders to recognize that developing a long-term mindset takes time and to be willing to work on building these skills over the long-term. By putting in the effort to develop a long-term mindset, traders can increase their chances of success and better navigate the challenges of the markets.

20 The Benefits of Financial Freedom: Why It's Worth Striving for

Financial freedom is a state of being in which one is able to meet their financial needs and goals without the constraints of a traditional job or fixed income. It is a state of independence and autonomy that allows individuals to live their lives on their own terms and pursue their passions and interests. There are many benefits to achieving financial freedom, and it is a goal worth striving for.

Time freedom:
One of the most significant benefits of financial freedom is the ability to have more control over one's time. With financial freedom, individuals are able to set their own schedules and prioritize their time according to their own values and goals. This can allow for a greater work-life balance and the opportunity to engage in activities outside of work that bring joy and fulfillment.

Having control over one's time can also allow for greater flexibility and the ability to pursue side hustles or other entrepreneurial ventures. It can provide the opportunity to take on projects and assignments that align with one's values and goals, rather than being constrained by the demands of a traditional job.

In addition to providing greater control over one's time, financial freedom can also allow for the opportunity to take extended time off or to travel and explore new places. It can provide the freedom to spend more time with loved ones and to pursue hobbies and interests that may have been neglected due to the demands of a traditional job.

Overall, time freedom is a key benefit of financial

freedom that allows individuals to live their lives on their own terms and to prioritize what is most important to them.

Location freedom:
Financial freedom also provides the opportunity for location freedom, or the ability to live and work from anywhere in the world. With the rise of remote work and the proliferation of digital technologies, it is now possible for many individuals to earn a living from anywhere with an internet connection. This can allow for greater flexibility and the opportunity to live in a location that aligns with one's values and goals.

Location freedom can provide the opportunity to live in a place with a lower cost of living, allowing for greater financial security and the ability to stretch one's income further. It can also provide the opportunity to live in a location with a higher quality of life, such as a location with a desirable climate or access to recreational activities.

In addition to providing greater control over where one lives, location freedom can also allow for the opportunity to travel and experience new places. It can provide the freedom to live a nomadic lifestyle and to explore different parts of the world on a longer-term basis.

Overall, location freedom is a key benefit of financial freedom that allows individuals to live and work from anywhere in the world and to pursue a lifestyle that aligns with their values and goals.

Financial security:
Achieving financial freedom also provides a greater level of financial security. By building up a substantial financial cushion and having multiple streams of income, individuals are better able to weather financial challenges and unexpected expenses. Financial freedom can provide peace

of mind and the ability to focus on what truly matters rather than worrying about financial security.

Having financial security can allow individuals to take risks and pursue opportunities that may not be possible with a traditional job and fixed income. It can provide the freedom to invest in oneself and to pursue entrepreneurial ventures or other opportunities that align with one's values and goals.

In addition to providing a sense of security and stability, financial freedom can also allow for the opportunity to retire earlier or to work on a part-time basis. It can provide the freedom to choose when and how to work, rather than being constrained by the demands of a traditional job.

Overall, financial security is a key benefit of financial freedom that allows individuals to have peace of mind and the ability to focus on what truly matters, rather than worrying about financial security. It can provide the freedom to take risks and pursue opportunities that align with one's values and goals.

Personal growth:
Financial freedom can also provide opportunities for personal growth and development. With the ability to set one's own schedule and priorities, individuals can pursue learning and growth opportunities that align with their passions and goals. This can lead to greater personal fulfillment and a sense of purpose.

Having the freedom to pursue one's passions and interests can lead to greater satisfaction and fulfillment in life. It can provide the opportunity to try new things and to engage in activities that bring joy and meaning.

In addition to providing opportunities for personal

growth and development, financial freedom can also allow for the opportunity to give back and make a positive impact in the world. It can provide the freedom to volunteer or to engage in charitable activities that align with one's values and goals.

Overall, personal growth is a key benefit of financial freedom that allows individuals to pursue learning and growth opportunities that align with their passions and goals and to find greater fulfillment and purpose in life.

Increased opportunities:
Another benefit of financial freedom is the increased opportunities it can provide. With financial freedom, individuals are able to take on new projects and opportunities that may not be possible with a traditional job and fixed income. It can provide the freedom to pursue entrepreneurial ventures or to invest in oneself through education or other personal development opportunities.

Having financial freedom can also allow for the opportunity to relocate for a new job or career opportunity. It can provide the flexibility to pursue opportunities that may not be available in one's current location.

In addition to providing increased opportunities for work and career growth, financial freedom can also provide the opportunity to travel and experience new places. It can provide the freedom to take extended vacations or to live a nomadic lifestyle and explore different parts of the world.

Overall, increased opportunities is a key benefit of financial freedom that allows individuals to pursue new projects and opportunities that align with their values and goals and to experience new things.

Improved relationships:

Financial freedom can also lead to improved relationships with loved ones. With the ability to set one's own schedule and priorities, individuals are able to spend more quality time with loved ones and to prioritize their relationships. This can lead to stronger and more meaningful connections with family and friends.

Having financial freedom can also provide the opportunity to support loved ones financially, whether it be through gifts or financial assistance in times of need. It can provide the freedom to give back and to make a positive impact on the lives of others.

Overall, improved relationships is a key benefit of financial freedom that allows individuals to prioritize their relationships and to make a positive impact on the lives of loved ones.

Overall, financial freedom provides many benefits, including time freedom, location freedom, financial security, personal growth, increased opportunities, and improved relationships. By striving for financial freedom, individuals can live their lives on their own terms and pursue their passions and interests with greater independence and autonomy. It is a goal worth striving for due to the many benefits it can provide.